SAVING EARTH'S BIOMES

RESTORING THE GREAT LAKES

by Ben McClanahan

FOCUS
READERS.

NAVIGATOR

WWW.FOCUSREADERS.COM

Focus Readers is distributed by North Star Editions:
sales@northstareditions.com | 888-417-0195

Produced for Focus Readers by Red Line Editorial.

Content Consultant: Peter McIntyre, Associate Professor, Cornell University

Photographs ©: csterken/iStockphoto, cover, 1; AJKamps/Shutterstock Images, 4–5; Rainer Lesniewski/Shutterstock Images, 7; Detroit Publishing Co./Library of Congress, 9, 18–19; corfoto/iStockphoto, 10–11; Haraz N. Ghanbari/AP Images, 13; Jnlyl/Shutterstock Images, 15; Gena Melendrez/Shutterstock Images, 17; Bettmann/Getty Images, 21; narvikk/iStockphoto, 23; Brett Billings/US Fish and Wildlife Service, 24–25; Jeff Schmaltz/MODIS Rapid Response Team/GSFC/NASA, 27; Joshua Stevens/MODIS/NASA EOSDIS/LANCE and GIBS/Worldview/NASA, 29

Library of Congress Cataloging-in-Publication Data
Names: McClanahan, Ben, 1978- author.
Title: Restoring the Great Lakes / by Ben McClanahan.
Description: Lake Elmo : Focus Readers, [2020] | Series: Saving earth's
   biomes | Includes index. | Audience: Grades 4-6
Identifiers: LCCN 2019031733 (print) | LCCN 2019031734 (ebook) | ISBN
   9781644930700 (hardcover) | ISBN 9781644931493 (paperback) | ISBN
   9781644933077 (pdf) | ISBN 9781644932285 (ebook)
Subjects: LCSH: Lake restoration--Great Lakes (North America)--Juvenile
   literature.
Classification: LCC SH157.85.L34 M33 2020 (print) | LCC SH157.85.L34
   (ebook) | DDC 333.91/631530977--dc23
LC record available at https://lccn.loc.gov/2019031733
LC ebook record available at https://lccn.loc.gov/2019031734

Printed in the United States of America
Mankato, MN
012020

ABOUT THE AUTHOR

Ben McClanahan has always been curious about science, nature, and the world around us. Writing books has allowed him to explore a wide variety of people and places.

TABLE OF CONTENTS

CHAPTER 1

A GREAT HISTORY

From shore, the Great Lakes appear to be oceans. Each of these five lakes stretches farther than the eye can see. The Great Lakes form the largest body of fresh water on Earth. Together, they cover 94,000 square miles (244,000 sq km). They hold 21 percent of all the liquid fresh water on Earth's surface.

The water in the Great Lakes could cover the United States nearly 10 feet (3.0 m) deep.

The Great Lakes support a unique **ecosystem**. More than 3,500 **species** of plants and animals live in the Great Lakes area. More than 150 of the species are fish, including sturgeon, walleye, and bass. In addition, more than 30 million people call the area home. Millions more depend on the lakes for clean drinking water.

People have lived in the Great Lakes region for more than 10,000 years. Before European settlers came, **Indigenous** Peoples developed an active **economy** there. They fished throughout the area. They hunted, too. However, they kept the ecosystem healthy.

In the 1600s, European settlers came to the Great Lakes area. These people cut down the forests for wood. Then they used the land for farming. Without as many trees, the land began to wear away.

GREAT LAKES REGION

As a result, a lot of **sediment** began entering the area's rivers. That sediment flowed into the lakes. Farm chemicals also began washing into the lakes.

Over time, settlers built large cities around the Great Lakes. Beginning in the

INDIGENOUS PEOPLES

Approximately 100 groups of Indigenous Peoples live in the Great Lakes area. Many of them care for nature as an important part of their cultures. For example, Josephine Mandamin was a member of the Wikwemikong First Nation in Ontario, Canada. Before her death in 2019, she made "water walks" around all of the Great Lakes. In total, she walked more than 10,600 miles (17,000 km). These walks raised awareness about helping the Great Lakes.

Near Lake Erie, the city of Ecorse, Michigan, was home to a lot of the country's shipping industry in the early 1900s.

1800s, they built factories and power plants. A large amount of waste began entering the lakes. In addition, many **introduced species** started to enter the lakes. These changes harm the animals and plants of the Great Lakes.

CHAPTER 2

THREATS TO THE GREAT LAKES

Today, the Great Lakes face many dangers. Introduced species are one of the lakes' major problems. Ships sometimes introduce these species by accident. Other times, people introduce them on purpose for fishing. Since the 1800s, at least 25 species of non-native fish have entered the Great Lakes.

Zebra mussels are one of the most harmful introduced species in the Great Lakes.

11

Zebra mussels are one example of a harmful introduced species. These clam-like creatures feed on large amounts of algae in the lakes. Algae are very tiny plants found in water. Many native animals depend on that algae for food. For reasons such as this, introduced species put the Great Lakes' **biodiversity** at risk.

Chemical pollution has greatly damaged the Great Lakes as well. Rainfall often washes waste into the lakes. Farm chemicals are one example of this waste. These chemicals pollute many people's drinking water. The waste can also be toxic to plants and animals. It can build

Of all the Great Lakes, algae blooms tend to hit Lake Erie the hardest.

up in fish's bodies. As a result, some types of fish are not safe for people to eat.

Some farm chemicals also cause more algae to grow in the lakes. When algae die, they fall to the bottom of the water. Then they rot. This process can lower the amount of oxygen in the water. Fish and other species need oxygen to survive.

This problem is especially bad for animals in Lake Erie.

Finally, **climate change** is causing major problems for the Great Lakes. Over the last 100 years, most lakes on Earth have gotten warmer on average. The water is becoming too warm for some

PLASTIC IN THE LAKES

More than 22 million pounds (100 million kg) of plastic enters the Great Lakes each year. Over time, this plastic breaks down into tiny pieces. These pieces are called microplastics. They are too small to see. In water, they absorb harmful chemicals and bacteria. These plastics sometimes get into drinking water. Fish also eat the plastic by mistake. As a result, people may eat or drink dangerous plastic.

plants and animals. In addition, warm water holds less oxygen. It also causes more algae to form. These changes harm native plants and animals. They also hurt businesses, such as fishing, that depend on the lakes.

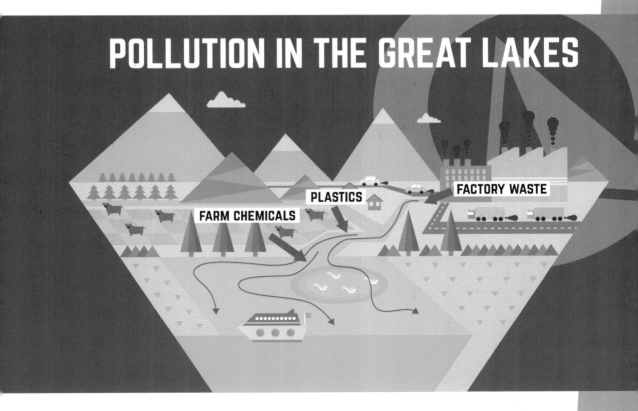

POLLUTION IN THE GREAT LAKES

PLASTICS

FARM CHEMICALS

FACTORY WASTE

SEA LAMPREYS

Sea lampreys are an introduced species in the Great Lakes. They are native to the Atlantic Ocean. People first noticed the fish in Lake Ontario in 1835. In the 1900s, the fish spread through shipping waterways. In the next few decades, its numbers increased in all the lakes.

During its life, a sea lamprey can kill up to 40 pounds (18 kg) of large fish. First, a lamprey attaches to another fish. Then, it sucks that fish's blood and other fluids. Lamprey numbers can also grow quickly. One female lamprey can lay up to 100,000 eggs.

Sea lampreys are one of the most harmful animals in the Great Lakes. Before their arrival, approximately 15 million pounds (6.8 million kg) of lake trout was caught each year. By the 1960s, this amount was down to only 300,000 pounds

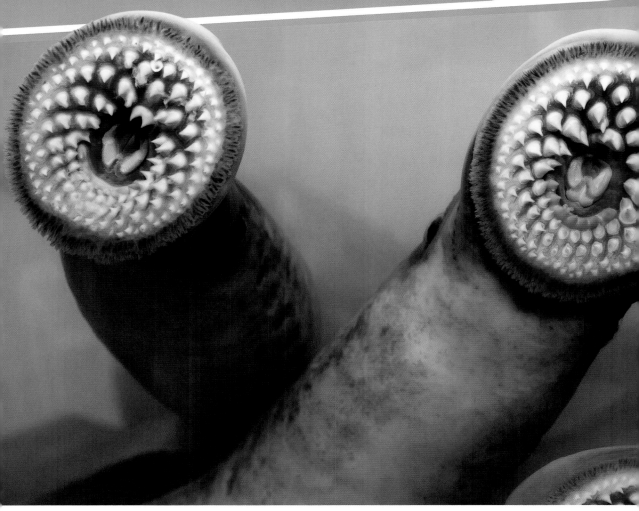

Sea lampreys do not have jaws. They use suction cup mouths and rings of sharp teeth to stick to larger fish.

(136,000 kg) per year. Overfishing and lampreys caused this change. Governments are trying to control how many lampreys are in the lakes. They hope to improve fishing opportunities.

CHAPTER 3

PROTECTING THE WATERS

Cities grew around the Great Lakes during the 1800s. During this time, pollution began to cause problems. For example, people in Chicago depended on drinking water from Lake Michigan. But the Chicago River brought a lot of the city's waste into the lake. As a result, the water became unsafe to drink.

A ship travels along the Chicago River during the early 1900s.

In the 1890s, city officials worked to turn the flow of the Chicago River around. The river now flows away from the lake. Still, a large amount of pollution was entering the Great Lakes. And governments did little to stop the problem. But a major event helped change the future of the lakes.

The Cuyahoga River flows into Lake Erie. For many years, it was one of the dirtiest rivers in the United States. A lot of waste poured into the river. Then the waste flowed into Lake Erie. In 1969, chemicals in the river caught fire. This fire was not the first. Since 1869, the river had caught fire 13 times. However,

One of the worst fires on the Cuyahoga River occurred in 1952.

news of the 1969 fire appeared across the country on TV. The event helped many people understand the dangers of water pollution.

The 1969 fire helped win support for the Clean Water Act in 1972. This act was the first US law to address water pollution. The law was important for cleaning up the Great Lakes. Businesses had to limit their pollution of rivers and lakes. Cities had to pollute less, too. The law also set basic standards for water safety. People could no longer dump chemicals straight into the lakes. They were not allowed to dump garbage either. A US agency helped make sure these new rules were followed.

Canada and the United States also signed the Great Lakes Quality Agreement in 1972. The agreement is still

Until the Clean Water Act in 1972, factories could legally dump waste straight into bodies of water.

working today. It includes rules against introducing new species. The agreement also sets a clear goal of guarding native plants and animals. In these ways and others, it tries to limit harm to the Great Lakes area.

CHAPTER 4

LOOKING AHEAD

Efforts to protect and restore the Great Lakes region are starting to show benefits. Many species' numbers have stopped going down. Some are even going up. For example, lake sturgeon numbers have become stable in several rivers. People are also returning sturgeon to areas where they had disappeared.

Researchers for the US Fish and Wildlife Service release lake sturgeon back into water.

In 2009, the United States started the Great Lakes Restoration Initiative. This program helped prevent 800,000 pounds (363,000 kg) of waste from entering the lakes. In addition, Canada started Ontario's Great Lakes Strategy in 2012. One of this plan's goals is to guard lake shores. Another goal is to cut pollution. The plan improved drinking water quality.

Scientists continue to learn about the Great Lakes. For example, some scientists use satellites to create maps of algae populations. The maps are based on how green the water looks from space. The maps suggest places where reducing pollution is most important.

LAKE ERIE

Algae blooms on Lake Erie have gotten so bad that they are visible from space.

Scientists are also studying how to address climate change. This problem is already affecting the lakes and will likely become worse. For instance, ice forms on the surface of the lakes during winter.

However, the ice is forming later than it used to. The ice is melting earlier, too. In addition, algae blooms are creating low oxygen on the bottom of Lake Erie. This problem is happening for the first time in decades.

TRACKING FISH

Scientists use many tools to understand fish behavior. One type of tool uses sound-making tags. These tags help scientists track fish. First, the scientists catch certain fish. They place a small tag inside each fish's body. Then, they return the fish to the water. The tags send out brief sounds. After receiving these signals, scientists can learn where those fish live. This way, they learn which areas need to be protected in order to grow fish populations.

The Great Lakes thaw after the winter of 2018–19.

The dangers to the Great Lakes are far from over. Pollution continues to enter the lakes. Climate change will become more extreme. And new threats will come. But millions of people care about the Great Lakes. These people are trying to help to protect them.

FOCUS ON
RESTORING THE GREAT LAKES

Write your answers on a separate piece of paper.

1. Write a sentence that describes how introduced species have been harmful to the Great Lakes.

2. What are the most important actions you can take to help improve the health of the lakes?

3. The Great Lakes contain how much of the planet's fresh water?

    A. 5 percent
    B. 21 percent
    C. 73 percent

4. Why are some fish from the Great Lakes unsafe for people to eat?

    A. They are dangerous to catch.
    B. They contain high levels of dangerous chemicals.
    C. They are naturally dangerous to eat.

Answer key on page 32.

GLOSSARY

biodiversity
The number of different species that live in an area.

climate change
A human-caused global crisis involving long-term changes in Earth's temperature and weather patterns.

economy
A system of goods, services, money, and jobs.

ecosystem
A community of living things and how they interact with their surrounding environment.

indigenous
Native to a region, or belonging to ancestors who did not immigrate to the region.

introduced species
Plant and animal species brought to an ecosystem by people instead of developing as part of the ecosystem.

sediment
Tiny soil particles, sand, or other materials that are carried by flowing water, wind, or ice.

species
A group of animals or plants that share the same body shape and can breed with one another.

TO LEARN MORE

BOOKS

Amstutz, Lisa J. *Bringing Back Our Freshwater Lakes*. Minneapolis: Abdo Publishing, 2018.

Brundle, Harriet. *Pollution*. New York: KidHaven Publishing, 2018.

Sawyer, Ava. *Humans and the Hydrosphere: Protecting Earth's Water Sources*. North Mankato, MN: Capstone Press, 2018.

NOTE TO EDUCATORS

Visit **www.focusreaders.com** to find lesson plans, activities, links, and other resources related to this title.

INDEX

Answer Key: **1.** Answers will vary; **2.** Answers will vary; **3.** B; **4.** B